# TOP TIPS:
# EXPLORING THE BIBLE
# WITH YOUNG PEOPLE

Terry Clutterham and John Stephenson

Copyright © Scripture Union 2009
First published 2009
ISBN 978 184427 336 2

Scripture Union England and Wales
207-209 Queensway, Bletchley, Milton
Keynes, MK2 2EB, England
Email: info@scriptureunion.org.uk
Website: www.scriptureunion.org.uk

Scripture Union Australia
Locked Bag 2, Central Coast Business
Centre, NSW 2252
Website: www.scriptureunion.org.au

Scripture Union USA
PO Box 987, Valley Forge, PA 19482
Website: www.scriptureunion.org

Scripture quotations are taken from
the HOLY BIBLE, TODAY'S NEW
INTERNATIONAL VERSION (TNIV),
©2004 by International Bible Society.
Used by permission of Hodder &
Stoughton, a division of Hodder
Headline Ltd. All rights reserved.

The right of Terry Clutterham and
John Stephenson to be identified as
authors of this work has been
asserted by them in accordance with
the Copyright, Designs and Patents
Act 1988.

British Library Cataloguing-in-
Publication Data: a catalogue record
of this book is available from the
British Library.

Printed and bound in Singapore by
Tien Wah Press Ltd

Logo, cover design, internal design:
www.splash-design.co.uk

Internal illustrations: Colin Smithson

Typesetting: Richard Jefferson,
Author & Publisher Services

Advisers: John Grayston, Nathan Iles,
John Marshall

Scripture Union is an
international Christian charity working
with churches in more than 130
countries, providing resources to bring
the good news about Jesus Christ to
children, young people and families
and to encourage them to develop
spiritually through the Bible and
prayer.

As well as our network of volunteers,
staff and associates who run holidays,
church-based events and school
Christian groups, we produce a wide
range of publications and support
those who use our resources through
training programmes.

# CONTENTS

# INTRODUCTION

Young people from many different countries all around the world were together at an International Camp. We were working together in constructing a giant Bible timeline, placing on the line the key characters and events from Bible history. We explored art pictures of biblical stories and worked out where these too should be placed. The playing field became the map of the Middle East in biblical times with markers to show the journeys that God's people took and the places Jesus and Paul visited.

The climax came when the map and timeline were widened and lengthened as the story of the growth of Christianity in the young people's own countries were positioned on the line. Pictures and descriptions of both distant and recent history were spread out, from New Testament times until today. Communicating across cultural barriers and worshipping together in different languages was a powerful reminder of the theme so clearly illustrated on the time line: One Story – One People.

For all of us, including many young people, the challenge of exploring the Bible is 'Where do I start?' It's a big book – a veritable library all on its own with more pages than most textbooks, usually with no illustrations and set out in small print in columns. When we open it, we discover that it is set in a very different world to our own. The people, customs, rules, ideas and stories seem far removed from life in the twenty-first century! It's not surprising that faced with those problems many of us, not just young people, give up before we even start.

Exploring the Bible begins with remembering what the Bible shows us about God and people like you and me. The Bible is essentially about God's relationship with the universe, creation and people. It shows us what we could never hope to discover alone. God continues to be intimately involved with the world. He created us and gave us the responsibility of taking care of the world. He calls people everywhere to live in a relationship with him and to join in with his great plan of restoring his creation.

We explore the Bible not to become more knowledgeable or to pass an exam. It is not about head knowledge. Instead God invites us to get to know him, the author. In doing so, we will discover what plans God has for our lives, the people we live with, the places we live in and the world we are called to enjoy and care for. It's an adventure that is far more exciting than any other. It is what God intended.

One reason why we may find it hard is that we often begin looking at the Bible with a magnifying glass and get lost in the detail of the words. We need to step back, to see the Bible as one big story with God as the main character. What is he doing in the world? How is he influencing events? Patterns and plans begin to emerge.

One way of thinking of the big story of the Bible is by taking the analogy of a symphony with four movements. Themes and melodies are introduced and then reappear. This symphony is one piece but has four distinct movements: Creation and fall, God's people Israel, Jesus, and the Church. Themes that recur throughout the Bible help us to see how it is all connected. As we explore each movement, we need to remember where it fits in the overall story. This is what the young people at the International Camp discovered in such a tangible and faith-shaping way.

God has called you to equip the young people in your care to open up the Bible for themselves so that together you can be amazed at how the Bible story consistently moves towards the fulfilment of God's plan. Although written for youth workers, most of the principles within this book are relevant for those working with children or adults!

# 1

# PART ONE –
# CLUES FROM THE BIBLE

To understand the Bible, God's Word, we need to have a clear idea about what it contains and why it is relevant. It is important to remember that the Bible is written in a variety of styles of literature. These form the basis of the following 'clues'. (The different styles of literature are emboldened below.)

## God's Word was...

## ... to be at the heart of life

God's Word was found in Old Testament **history**. The first five books of the Bible, called the Pentateuch, are often referred to as the Law. These books show the way in which God was active in the history of his people. He chose them and rescued them. But being chosen by God meant that God's people had responsibilities. Moses told the people, 'These commandments ... are to be on your hearts ... Talk about them when you sit at home and when you walk along the road, when you lie down and when you get up' (Deuteronomy 6:6,7). When Joshua succeeded Moses, God commanded him to make sure that he gave the law his full attention: 'Keep this Book of the Law always on your lips; meditate on it day and night, so that you may be careful to do everything written in it' (Joshua 1:8).

## ... to be cherished

God's Word was found in Old Testament **poetry**. Take Psalm 119:105 'Your word is a lamp to my feet and a light for my path'. This longest of all psalms in the Bible is made up of 176 verses of meditation on the importance of God's Word to the life of the psalmist. There is a passion to know God's Word and a desire to obey it. If we are to teach the

Bible to others, we ourselves need that love for God's Word that is exemplified here and anticipate that it will blossom in others.

**Think about...**
Talk with other youth workers about how you can foster in yourselves that same passion for God's Word shown by the psalmist and then encourage it among the young people you work with.

## ... for today and the future

God's Word was found in Old Testament **prophecy**. The prophets were given the responsibility of communicating God's message to the people for their particular time and place. But they also spoke their message in the light of God's bigger, future plan of redemption. For example, Isaiah and Jeremiah consistently pointed the people forward to a future time when God would act to bring about restoration, long after they were dead. These words were a precious source of hope to the people at the time and are a reminder of God's sovereignty in history.

**Think about...**
What would it mean to the young people you know for God's Word to be part of life, in the same way as eating is part of living? Eugene Peterson's book about the Bible, entitled *Eat this Book: a conversation in the art of spiritual reading*, picked up on this image from the prophets – see page 32.

## ... to be identified with and obeyed

God's Word from the Old Testament was very evident in the ministry of Jesus, as told in the **gospels**. When Jesus announced his ministry in the synagogue at Nazareth he quoted the words of the prophet Isaiah 'The Spirit of the Lord is on me ... '(Luke 4:18). In doing so, he demonstrated his link with the story of the past. He wanted people to see that his arrival and ministry was the continuation of what God had been doing throughout history and he submitted to it. With the words of scripture he overcame temptation by the devil (Luke 4:4,8,12). He quoted the psalmist as he cried out on the cross to his father (Psalm 22:1; Matthew 27:46). His instructions to his disciples were a constant reminder that the requirement of God's people was to obey God's Word. 'You are my friends if you do what I command' (John 15:14).

## ... to equip God's people

God's Word was evident in the writing of the **epistles**. Paul advised Timothy, as a church leader, to emphasise the importance of teaching the Bible to others and equipping them to do the same (2 Timothy 1:13; 2:2). In this same letter, he summed up the role that scripture is to play in life and work:

> But as for you, continue in what you have learned and have become convinced of, because you know those from whom you learned it, and how from infancy you have known the Holy Scriptures, which are able to make you wise for salvation through faith in Christ Jesus. All Scripture is God-breathed and is useful for teaching, rebuking, correcting and training in righteousness, so that all God's people may be thoroughly equipped for every good work (2 Timothy 3:14–17).

The impact of God's Word on our lives is fourfold:

- Relationship – God's Word makes us 'wise for salvation', being restored in our relationship with God.
- Teaching – God's Word increases our understanding of who God is and how he wants us to live.
- Transformation – God's Word reveals areas of life that need to change for anyone to live a righteous life.
- Service – God's Word equips us to serve him.

**In reality…**

Psalm 46:7 says 'The LORD Almighty is with us; the God of Jacob is our fortress'. After looking at this in the group, Julie drew a house. 'Why a house?' the leader asked. She replied, 'That's the women's refuge where we go on a Friday night to be safe when my father comes home drunk'. God's Word speaks to real situations in people's lives today, as well as in history.

## … God in action

When God speaks, things happen! Creation came into being through his Word. Hebrews 1 reminds us that God acts in history, but ultimately he has spoken and acted in his Son, Jesus. The Word became flesh and lived for a while among us (John 1:14). The Word of God is not a dead text only to be analysed and dissected. The Holy Spirit takes the text and speaks to us. 'For the word of God is alive and active … it judges the thoughts and attitudes of the heart' (Hebrews 4:12).

# 2

# PART TWO –
# BASIC GUIDELINES

## Making sense of the Bible

If we are to make sense of the Bible, we need some basic guidelines to help us understand what it means. Down through the ages, people have often twisted the Bible to support their own point of view, for example using Eve's response to the serpent to reinforce the image of all women as deceivers, or Noah's curse of Ham in Genesis 9 to support apartheid. It is not only a foolish thing to start with our own perspective rather than God's, but it is also a recipe for disaster. We can do this deliberately or it can be unconscious because we don't ask important questions such as these three that help us identify the meaning of any passage in the Bible:

*   What did the author intend?
*   What does the text actually say?
*   What do we understand it to mean now?

### Research the context

To get to the intention of the author we need to appreciate what the world was like when the words were recorded. Jesus told lots of stories using everyday analogies, but to grasp their full meaning we must know what the world was like when those words were spoken. How did people live? What was their situation? What sort of lives did they lead? For example, unless you know that Samaritans were religious outcasts, the parable of the good Samaritan is simply a story about helping others.

We also need to know where any one passage fits in the biblical story – what is going on in this part of the Bible, how does this story fit in the overall plan? The books of prophecy are not placed chronologically in the Bible so we need to know where they fit in the timeline of the Bible. This involves exploration and searching for information but this is essential for us and others to make sense of the Bible. Check out *Explorer's Guide to*

*the Bible*, John Grayston –
see page 32.

## Identify the genre

Many people have a favourite
type of writing – science fiction,
romance, biography. The Bible
has 66 books and they too have
different types of writing. It helps
to know what type (or genre) of writing we are reading. Is it
history or poetry, prophecy or wisdom, gospel or letters? Once we
know what type, then we are in a better position to grasp what the
words mean. For example, poetry will use imaginative language whilst
epistles contain denser pieces of writing and personal comments.

> **Think about...**
> Psalm 137 was written while the people
> of Israel were in exile in Babylon. Why
> would this song have been appropriate
> then? How does that help us understand
> its meaning today?

## Understand the ideas

The Bible was not written in English! People translating from Hebrew,
Aramaic or Greek find words that have an equivalent meaning. Sometimes
this means they use words that are no longer in common usage or where
the meaning is not clear or has even changed. Words such as fellowship,
covenant or redemption need to be examined to see what they mean if
we are going to grasp what the Bible actually says. Using different
translations can help to shed light on the meaning of the words.

## Extract the principles

Although the world has changed, God remains the same. We need to
look for the principles about him and his world that are in the text rather
than just taking the text itself at face value. Most people don't offer food
to idols (although in some parts of the world they do) yet Paul spends the
whole of chapter 8 of 1 Corinthians explaining what to do in that

situation. Are these words irrelevant for us today or do we dig deeper to unravel the truth behind Paul's words and then work out what this might mean in situations we face? To explore these ideas, read *Light to Live By: How to interpret the Bible*, Richard Briggs – see page 32.

## Making connections

Young people are generally interested in finding out about things that affect them. But young people are not all the same. Each is a unique individual with a different combination of interests, learning styles, family backgrounds and lots more besides. You will know only too well how important it is to treat them as individuals and encourage them to meet the God of the Bible for themselves.

### Group learning

Young people are used to working together. Challenge them to explore for themselves within their groups. Set challenges and problems to solve. Your job is not to give them the answers – instead design learning opportunities that allow discovery. Learning takes place as much in the research as it does in the conclusions reached.

### Different learning styles

Learning is not simply a case of listening and remembering. Visual (seeing), audio (hearing) and kinaesthetic (active) learning styles are relevant for all of us. To connect with young people we must allow for these different learning styles and design ways of connecting with the Bible that use all three approaches. For example, to help young people retell a Bible story, divide into three groups – one group draws the key events in the story as a comic strip (visual), one re-reads the story adding sound effects (audio), while the third re-enacts the story as a piece of drama (kinaesthetic). To explore this look at Chapter 5 of *Pretty much everything you need to know about working with 11–14s*, Tricia Williams and John Stephenson – see page 32.

**Think about...**
What is your preferred learning style? How can you make sure that learning styles other than your preferred one are included?

## Multi-sensory approaches

All five senses can be employed as we meet God through his Word. For example: use pictures and art; listen to music and to God's Word read or dramatised; use objects like stones and nails; taste salt and honey; smell perfume or oil burning. All of these approaches allow us to engage in deeper ways with God's Word. For more ideas read *Top Tips on Prompting prayer* by Sarah Bingham and Vicki Blyth – see inside front cover.

## Connecting with the whole person

God's desire is that we relate to him with the whole of our lives – intellectually, physically and emotionally. Create opportunities for young people to respond to God's Word in ways that allow them to connect with their heads, hearts and hands.

**In reality...**
Three young people were given £10 and asked to use it during the week to make money. The following week they reported back as the group looked at the parable of the talents. All the money raised went to charity.

## Making it relevant

In any group of young people there are those facing similar pressures. God's Word has an impact on any emotional, social, intellectual or physical issue, but young people may need convincing that the Bible is truly relevant to their daily life.

### At school

School is the most significant place of influence for young people. They spend more time there than in any other place. They face the issues of peer pressure and meet a range of differing opinions. Those who have a faith have to work out what it means to live for God at school. For those without a faith, this may be the first place where they encounter Christians.

The Bible offers surprisingly numerous examples of God's people living in situations students can identify with. The example of Daniel living as an exile in Babylon offers a clear example of someone living in a hostile environment which has values that oppose God's values. God's people were instructed to live distinctive lives that showed what God was like to the nations around them. Or take the way that the early church lived and shared the message of Jesus to those around them as their evangelism in words and deeds went hand in hand. Such examples can encourage young people to see that God can be relied upon in a variety of challenging situations.

The reliability of the Bible will be examined in RE lessons. We can help students to understand that the Bible is trustworthy, not just because it says it is, but because it is an accurate historical document. This means being

### Think about…

How does the way that you study the Bible together help young people in your care to live out their faith at school?

willing to examine the story of how the Bible came to us and how we know it can be trusted. To find out more, look at *The Story of the Book* by Terence Copley – see page 32.

## At home

Often it is with those who know us best that we find it hardest to be real about our faith. Sibling rivalry and generation gaps can make it tough to live out an authentic faith. The Bible speaks about the responsibility parents have for the spiritual nurture of children. The Passover meal is built around the story of God's redemption and is retold in the context of a family meal (Exodus 12). The Bible is full of stories about the problems and joys of family life, and gives plenty of practical principles, albeit against a different cultural background. Guiding young people to apply the Bible to their home situations will help them to see its relevance.

## At church

God calls us to be part of a new family, so reading the Bible together and meeting with others for prayer and worship are central activities. Young people have a key place in church life, not just as observers but as participants. Their perspective on God's Word benefits us all. They are as much the church of today as they are the church of tomorrow.

## At leisure

In a world of Playstations, iPods, multi-channel TV and numerous leisure options, it is easy for God's Word to be squeezed out. Rather than seeing the Bible in competition with these forms of leisure, look for ways to use technology that allow young people to connect with God's Word.

Go to www.wordlive.org for a flexible, multi-media approach to the Bible and encourage young people to bring the Bible into their technological world. Use social networking sites as spaces to share what you are learning with others in the group, and use websites to provide supporting background ideas and images that bring the Bible to life. Encourage young people to

**In reality...**

One church decided every evening service would be designed to make young people feel welcome with a mix of contemporary and traditional songs, video clips and visual meditation, space for discussion as part of the sermon and young people involved in leading prayer and reading the Bible. All gifts and skills were used for the benefit of everyone.

create and then share their own electronic photographic sequence to portray what a Bible verse means to them.

## Making groups work

Belonging is vitally important to young people. However creative our approach to the Bible may be, young people won't engage if they feel uncomfortable. Most of the time, a small group is the context in which they will encounter the Bible. It is vital to give time to getting this right.

## The environment

It is easier to concentrate in a relaxed setting so think about where your group meets. Is the seating comfortable? Can people see each other? Are there any distracting pictures or noises? Is it too warm or too cold? Getting these things right will make it more likely that young people will engage with the Bible. For more details, see *Top Tips on Leading small groups for children and young people* (SU).

## The group dynamics

In teenage years, peer pressure has a significant impact on how young people behave. Groups need to be small enough to allow everyone to contribute but large enough to allow people to choose to be observers. Generally we recommend groups of six to eight. Remember that some people speak first and think later, while others do the opposite. It is a real skill to be able to draw out quiet members and make sure that talkative members don't dominate. Here are some useful tips:

- Establish simple ground rules about listening to one another so that only one person speaks at a time.
- Praise the contributions of group members to encourage participation – to dismiss someone might cause them to 'clam up'.
- Allow the talkative ones to contribute but then draw in the opinions of others by asking what they think about the issue.
- Don't assume that not-speaking means not-participating – some people like to remain quiet in groups.
- Eye contact is invaluable to ensure everyone knows they are noticed and belong!

## The language

The Bible does contain some difficult ideas and concepts – don't ignore that. Take time to read from different translations to gain insight into what the words might mean. Explain theological ideas or background information in simple language and look for illustrations that connect with the world that young people live in.

## The questions

Sometimes young people don't contribute because questions seem trivial. Engagement with the text is not simply a matter of English comprehension. Devise open-ended questions that allow opinions to be expressed, making use of the pattern given on page 10. Why do you think David behaved like this? What do you think the disciples felt? How would you have responded if you were Peter? In doing this you will encourage young people to return afresh to the text to examine what is actually taking place.

## The application

Young people are keen to know how faith works for today. Don't stop at reading and studying the text. Think together about what action you might take in response. Be practical in thinking about how the Bible passage relates to the world they live in as well as aspirations for the future.

# PART THREE – PRACTICAL IDEAS

# 3

These practical ideas are divided into three parts
* Engage our lives with God's story
* Examine and retell stories in the Bible
* Explore the Big Story of the Bible

## Engage our lives with God's story

### Be an example
Young people will want to meet God through the Bible themselves if they catch our enthusiasm for it. We will do this as we share how God has spoken to us, give current examples of how we are responding to God's Word and are willing to admit when we struggle or can't give an answer to a question. Most young people learn from what they see so pray that God will speak to us by his Holy Spirit. Our love for the Bible will be infectious. One way of making space to personally engage with the Bible text is keeping a journal or on-line blog. Each day, record what strikes you in a short paragraph. Then when preparing to lead a session you can look back to see what challenged you in God's Word.

**Think about...**
How do you make time for God's Word in your schedule? How are you being transformed by what you read and hear?

### Listening to God's Word
It is easy to forget that for many centuries people could not read the Bible and in many parts of the world that is still true. Let your group listen, with their own Bibles closed, to the Bible being read from a less familiar translation such as the *New Living Translation* or *The Message*.

Ask God to speak then read the passage slowly and clearly. Talk together about whether there was a word or phrase that anyone noticed. Then ask them to read the passage on their own before talking about what it meant to them. Expect God to speak and allow the young people to share what he has said to them. As an alternative, listen to a recorded version of the Bible on CD.

### Lent Bible reading

Many young people give up chocolate for Lent but wouldn't think to deny themselves anything to give them more time for God. Challenge them to read a chapter of a Gospel each day. Share thoughts, questions and reflections by email or social networks and encourage one another to keep going. Provide a reading plan and keep in regular contact to encourage participants. Having established this pattern, encourage ongoing Bible reading to continue using regular Bible reading guides, printed or electronic.

### Bible memorisation

One way to make sure we understand the Bible and meditate on it is to memorise it. We want young people to fill their minds with God's Word. Launch a programme to remember key verses at a significant time such as New Year or as part of a Lent course. Don't be too ambitious but aim to learn 20 verses by heart over a set time.

### Lectio divina

This ancient practice of 'Praying the Bible' is a slow contemplative method, designed to ensure that we meditate and ruminate on God's Word. There are four stages:

- Lectio – reading. We read the scripture slowly, listening for the voice of God. As we do so a phrase or an idea is triggered.

- Meditatio – meditation. We next ponder on the words we have read taking time to consider their meaning.
- Oratio – prayer. We use the words we have been considering and turn them into a prayer of consecration to God.
- Contemplatio – contemplation. We simply remain silent resting in the presence of God and his words to us.

This is very different from the way in which most people encounter the Bible and will need practice and space if done as a group activity.

## Asking questions

If Bible exploration is to go further than simply head knowledge there are three distinctively different types of questions to be asked.

- Observation – searching for the facts: the who? what? where? when? and why? questions.
- Understanding – what do the words and phrases actually mean? How do I understand what it says?
- Application – actions to take? example to follow? command to obey? promise to remember?

## What question do you have?

As a group, read a passage of the Bible and then compile a list of five questions that are raised, based on the passage. Write these up, then spend the rest of the time exploring what insight the passage gives to the questions. Identify other parts of the Bible that help to find answers.

### 'Scribblearound'

Copy a Bible passage onto a piece of A4 paper and stick it onto a piece of flipchart paper. Give everyone a pen. After they have read the passage, ask people to ring any phrase that connects to something else and is prompted by the reading. It could be a song or hymn, another piece of the Bible, or simply the way that those particular verses make them feel (such as a wow!, a promise, a gulp!, a command). Use the completed sheet as a stimulus to prayer. This is especially a good way to respond personally to a complex piece of Paul's letters.

### Symbols method

This is a method used to explore the Bible together in small groups to encourage participation. It can be used with parables, psalms and many sections of the epistles. Write these six symbols on a piece of card to give to each person. After a time of reflection on a passage, share your observations.

    ↑ – something in these verses about Jesus or God
    ↓ – something in these verses about human nature
    🕯 – a new discovery made by reading these verses
    ! – the most exciting verse and why
    ? – anything not understood or that calls for exploration
    ← – a call for action made by these verses

Examples of passages you could use are: Psalm 104, 107, 139; Romans 8:1–17; Ephesians 2:1–18; Colossians 1:15–23;1 Peter 1:3–16; and parables in the Gospels.

### Make a model

Where the story has a clear sense of learning about God's character, provide everyone with a piece of air-drying clay to be shaped into something that reminds them about the aspect of God's character they have been considering. Talk about God as the models are shaped, or shape them in silence, followed by discussion.

## A postcard to God

To conclude a session, everyone writes a postcard to God expressing what they have learnt or been reminded of. Ask God to help you all do what he has challenged you about.

## Using objects

Often it is helpful to take away a reminder of the story your group has been considering. Look in the passage for examples that can be significant in symbolising the meaning of the passage. For example, Palm Sunday people take home a palm cross or a nail or small cross after thinking about the cross. Other examples include

taking away a bookmark, a pebble, a seed or a piece of card with
something significant written on it.

### Write a psalm

The psalms are the songbook of the Bible. They contain praise and
rejoicing but also pain and anguish. They are honest reflections of what
the people thought about life's events and God's part in their lives.
Rewriting a familiar psalm in your own words can be really valuable. Try
to use different analogies from the psalmist's by updating it. So 'The
Lord is my Shepherd' becomes 'The Lord is my ...'. Alternatively offer a
structure for a modern psalm such as:

> A sentence about an aspect of God's character
> Followed by a 'therefore' and a response that we might make
> Repeat the above two
> Something we would ask God to do for us
> Something we will do in response
> A concluding sentence of praise.

## Examine and retell stories in the Bible

As young people retell the powerful stories of the Bible they will
engage with the text and understand what it means. Learning takes
place as they work out how to retell it. Note that this is likely to appeal
most to active learners. Below are some examples of how to do that.

### Engage physically with the story

Many incidents in the Bible involve action. Jesus and the disciples
travelled a lot; the prophets built models and physically embodied their
message. As you think about a story ask 'What could young people do

to engage with this story?' 'What could they do or make?' Set them challenges to accomplish and problems to solve.

## Go to the place

Find places that echo the settings in the Bible and retell the story there. A beach, a courtyard, around a fire, up a mountain, in a boat, on a journey, over a meal… Examples include listening to the whole of the Sermon on the Mount on a hillside; reading at a city wall the story of Joshua at Jericho; reading Psalm 23 at a sheep farm; following the path of a stream from its source as you look at Ezekiel 47; visiting a vineyard as you look at John 15.

### In reality…

Living out the last 24 hours of the life of Jesus in an event called 'Being There' involves eating a Passover meal; walking and praying outside; lighting a fire and remembering Peter; re-enacting the trial of Jesus in a church at night; walking up a hill on Good Friday carrying a cross.

## What can you hear?

As you look at the Bible story, imagine what sounds there would be. Make a list of these, then retell the story adding sound effects to emphasise what is happening.

## Photo storyboard

Give a group a digital camera and a Bible story and ask the young people to construct and take six still photos to use to retell the story, transferring the images to a laptop. This is a good way to retell Jesus' parables or chunks of Bible history. If cameras are not available the group could create six freeze-frame moments as the story is retold, holding a pose for each moment.

### News reporter
Retell Bible stories as a news reporter at the scene. Either write and perform it as a live interview or film in advance to show as a news item. To offer a faithful report, the young people will have to engage with the Bible text.

### Chat Show
Imagine one of the characters in a Bible story is on a chat show, talking about their experience. Plan the chat show, choosing to do it in the style of a known presenter such as Jonathan Ross or Ricki Lake. Draw out the type of person this character is, what we know about them and how they will be presented in the chat show.

### Hold the front page
Design the front page of a newspaper with a headline, adverts, a picture and a main story. Use this as a tool to retell the main events of the story you are exploring.

### Dear Diary
Take one character in your story and write an imaginary diary entry for the day in question, retelling the story and including something about what the character felt.

## Update the parable

Many of Jesus' parables are set in places that are unfamiliar to twenty-first century urban city dwellers. Explore the parable dramatically by retelling it in a modern setting so that the story has the same impact as the one Jesus told. Not everyone is comfortable in using drama so it is important to have other ways of engaging with a story, such as drawing, using contemporary visual images or artefacts.

## How would you feel?

Look at a story from one of the Gospels or a story from Old Testament history. Ask each person to imagine themselves as one of the characters. Read the story and pause at different stages asking group members how they think their character would feel. This works best for stories with a number of characters and don't forget to include the unnamed spectators such as the disciples or the crowd.

## Paint the story

The Bible often uses word pictures to illustrate meaning. Jesus himself did this with his 'I am' sayings. The whole group or individuals represent the meaning of such an image using paint, crayons or coloured pencils. Alternatively create a collage using scrap materials, or a banner.

## Using artwork

For centuries the Bible has been a major source of inspiration for artists. Use such pictures to illustrate Bible stories. What is the artist trying to communicate? What insight does it give us to a Bible passage? What has the artist added or missed out?

Rembrandt's 'The
Return of the
Prodigal Son' and
Holman Hunt's 'The
Light of the World'
have been used
extensively for this purpose.

**Think about...**
With other youth workers, talk about
paintings that provoke insights for
meditating on God's word.

## Explore the Big Story of the Bible

### Connections
Collect verses from different parts of the Bible. Stick references around
the walls and ask young people to link them with wool or cotton. Use
different colours as follows: red for a quotation, yellow for a Bible
character, blue for a concept, idea, custom or theme. The room will
become a mass of colour to illustrate Bible connections.

### Timeline 1
Create a timeline using ribbon and card, going from 2000 BC to the
present day. Place the names of the best known characters throughout
history on the line. Every time you study the Bible, refer to this timeline
and add something to show where that story fits. This is all part of
God's one Big Story.

### Timeline 2
Write the main events of Bible history onto separate sheets of paper.
Ask the group to arrange these events in order on a washing line using
pegs. As an alternative collect pictures of key Bible events and place
them on a timeline. This often leads to good discussions as the young
people try to identify which story has been represented by the artist.
For details of Scripture Union's Bible Timeline see page 32.

## Geography

Never forget the geography of Bible lands. Some Bible stories only really make sense with a map. Either visualise a region or use labels on sticks to indicate location or journeys. For example: the Exodus, the exile, the ministry of Jesus, Paul's journeys. If you are following a series, roll out lino or thick paper or wallpaper on the floor with a map drawn on it to keep track of what is happening each week.

## Mini-Bible

Create a Bible pack by writing each book of the Bible on separate slips of paper. Arrange the young people in groups of three or four and share out a Bible pack between every three groups. Each group acquires what they think is the best mini-Bible by bartering with other groups. When they have finished talk about what books were important and which were least important, giving their reasons. These questions are what those translating the Bible for the first time had to think about. (This is based on a game from *Everyone's a Winner*: Bible Society).

**Think about...**
Which bits of the Bible do you study? Do you only read your favourite passages or do you also make sure you read the less well known parts?

## Bible cover

Imagine you are a marketing company with responsibility for designing a new Bible cover. In groups, come up with a new title, a strapline for the cover and a brief description for the back of the book. Give the group large paper and coloured pens to design their own cover. Talk about whether the cover of a Bible does or does not make a difference to how anyone uses a Bible.

### This is your life

Looking at the life of a Bible character can help draw together different parts of Bible history. This is especially important when we consider books that are not arranged chronologically. Take time to look at a character to see how their story develops. Many Old Testament characters offer fascinating insights and there are major characters in Acts who rarely get a mention. For example, Timothy and Barnabas are key characters mentioned over 20 times in the New Testament.

### Word study

It is helpful to see how an idea develops throughout the Bible. Preparing for this can take some time but online resources make the task easier. Choose an idea like 'grace' or 'redeem' and do a keyword search in an online Bible. If that proves too large, limit which books of the Bible you look at. Compile a list of appropriate verses and give them to the group. Together they can explore the verses and summarise what they teach about the significance of that idea in the Bible.

### Think about...

Colin Greene and Martin Robinson in their recent book, *Metavista: Bible, Church and Mission in an Age of Imagination, the Church after Postmodernity* (Paternoster Press) 2008, suggest four pairs of central themes in scripture. Creation and Covenant; Election and Exile; Imaging and Idolatry; Nations and Empire. These pairings provide useful themes for looking thematically at the Big Story of the Bible. What other themes could you use?

# TEN TOP TIPS

- Remember that God has given us the Bible so that we might have a relationship with him.

- Ensure your passion for God's Word and its effect on you is evident so that it infects the young people you work with.

- Think of the Bible as one story and read smaller sections with reference to the whole story.

- Approach the Bible as a learner, expecting God to speak *through* young people as well as to them.

- Encourage questions that go beyond knowledge so that the Bible is understood for life today.

- Allow space for reflection and meditation on God's Word – don't be afraid of silence.

- Use a variety of methods to engage all learning styles and all senses in Bible exploration.

- Allow time to apply the message of the Bible to the lives of young people by helping them to develop Bible handling skills for themselves.

- Encourage the habit of regular Bible reading and provide tools to make that easier.

- Pray that the Holy Spirit will work through his Word so that young people's lives might be transformed and they might be equipped to serve God.

# RESOURCES

## The Bible for young people

Andy Croft and Mike Pilavachi, *Storylines: tracing threads that run through the Bible*, Survivor, 2008

Whitney T Kuniholm, *Essential 100: Your way into the heart of the Bible*, Scripture Union, 2004

Vaughan Roberts, *God's Big Picture: Tracing the story-line of the Bible*, IVP, 2003

Heather Butler, *The 10 Must Know Stories*, Scripture Union, 2008

Robert Harrison, *Must Know Stories*, Scripture Union, 2008

*Word Up: Group Bible Study for 11–14s*, Scripture Union, 2004

*www.wordlive.org* by Scripture Union

*Bible Max* (two titles - Bible reading at your own pace), Scripture Union, 2007

## The Bible in youth ministry

Terry Clutterham, *The Adventure Begins*, Scripture Union/CPAS, 1996

Kathryn Copsey and Jean Elliott, *Top Tips on Communicating God in non-book ways*, Scripture Union, 2008

Terry Clutterham and John Stephenson, *Top Tips on Discovering the Bible with children*, Scripture Union, 2009

Terence Copley, *The Story of the Book*, Scripture Union, 2005

'Tricia Williams and John Stephenson, *Pretty much everything you need to know about working with 11–14s*, Scripture Union, 2004

John Stott, *Understanding the Bible*, Scripture Union, 2003

Eugene Peterson, *Eat this Book: a conversation in the art of spiritual reading*, Hodder & Stoughton, 2006

Richard Briggs, *Light to Live By: How to interpret the Bible*, Scripture Union, 2005

John Grayston, *Explorer's Guide to the Bible*, Scripture Union, 2008

Rachel Coupe, *Bible Timeline*, Scripture Union, 2008

## Bible study resources

Terry Clutterham, *Absolutely Everything*, Scripture Union, 2000

*SUbstance: Creation! Ten Bible-based sessions for your 14 to 18 youth group*, Scripture Union, 2008 (one of a series of six)